One for Words

By
Raja Zahid Khan

Poetry

One for Words

Copyright © 2020 Raja Zahid Khan

All rights reserved. No part of this publication may be produced, distributed, or transmitted in any form or by any means, including photocopying, recording, or other electronic or mechanical methods, without the prior written permission of the publisher, except in the case of brief quotations embodied in critical reviews and certain other non-commercial uses permitted by copyright law.

First Printed in United Kingdom 2020

Published by Conscious Dreams Publishing
www.consciousdreamspublishing.com

Edited by Daniella Blechner

ISBN: 978-1-913674-04-5

Dedication

You picked me up to the sky when I was feeling low,
Lifted me up and said let's go,
Raised me up to be with hard efforts,
Despite what you went through in your own life,
Not always did we agree,
Yet I loved you unconditionally,
May The Lord bless you Eternally.
My Father You believed in me,
Now, this is for You.

Contents

My Own Outlook 6
For the Youth Today 8
Search for a Brighter Day 10
Relations 13
People 16
The Streetz 18
Eternal Seeds 20
What Do We Do? 22
Parents 25
Look at How We Be 28
People Part ll 31
Times We Are Living In 34
Ask yourself 37
About the Author 39

My Own Outlook

The world is coming close,
can't get enough of its dose,
occupied in every sense,
the impact it has is immense,
blinded to see the sense,
or is it ignorance that's leading the line
for us time and time again,
as we maintain for worldly gain,
as some nations just wanting to remain,
still we breath and are left with a chance
to rectify our scales to reach a balance,
for we are living in sin,
not seeking forgiveness or giving thanks,
can't look out nor can we look within,
stuck in a zone, driven by other people's actions
even though we all stand alone,
we still don't feel at home or in ease,
carry it on by saying please,
ignorantly as we stumble again as quick as a swift breeze,
our hearts filled with disease,
not assisting our decisions through times like these.

Back at the same block, from here to there,
as time ticks forget to check our clock,
rusted and dusted like a cellar lock.

Where do we look or turn?
got to show self-concern,
some of us return,

learn from mistakes and errors to learn,
looking to see what we can earn,
others are headed in a direction
that'll leave them spinning in sections.

Material temptations leading us away,
so how do we be true to others around us
in a form of inspiration,
when we ourselves are suffering from a form of deprivation?
leading to misguiding another for whatever reason
they are still our brothers and sisters.

Life holds a key it lies with the Lord, the Creator of all,
guidance and piety is what you should pray for
in whatever way you pray,
in your search for better days,
wake up open your eyes and mind,
before you end up blinded to remain behind,
for you have time to make your living
to feel a feeling of true content,
a true bliss, without a need to resent,
think only the one true Lord above us all,
has the bliss, so find that,
the Lord, is the only way you will score,
to ever reach close to those heavenly doors.

Times like these people do as they please,
no soul wants to reflect on how they be, what will it be,
devote your hearts and minds
or you will lose your part to remain behind,
well before you leave us and this,
times near can you dismiss.

For the Youth Today

Watch what you do or where you go,
in time you want to know where you be,
chilling with people yet you don't see,
will it end up where you suffer?
fake friends soon flee,
use you when they are in need,
put you aside when they feel,
want to know when you when you cut the deal,
spending on them takes their appeal,
buying their meals, driving them round in your wheels,
up front in your face, like you brothers indeed,
together we will succeed.

You buy the line, it will reveal with time,
times are not what they used to be,
fake friends are no help to me.

Time passes by, everything is for a reason
father stressing over a son,
yet the son wants his fun, get to know limitation,
that will save you from times of deprivation,
getting involved heavy in what you do not know,
can hinder your progress carry on you
will know or find another place to go.

True brothers show some consideration,
show you a way,
a guide will not hold back
like brothers arrogant with pride,

with them they will not just push you aside,
nor will you feel pressurised,
won't aid you to sway will help you
those who are true, not turn away.

My message to you remain true to you and those around,
keep your feet steady on the ground,
think, be smart, work on things that benefit and build,
getting off track will block what you will
inside your heart and mind,
for slowly falling apart can leave you with eyes to see,
yet you have been blinded do try
if you don't you just pend on behind,
later asking why give things a shot,
you may miss on one but do not lose the will to carry on,
don't prolong listening to the same song,
there is always another chance to take,
don't be hard on yourself you will get that break,
try to put in effort and you will gain,
be patient, maintain,
for what is letting you down refrain,
stay away from that which destructive
you will threaten everything.
for these lines took thought and time,
hoping it reaches you fine,
no when to draw the line,
you will know when to mix and combine,
finding your flow,
for then you will know,
it is all in your own time.

Search for a Brighter Day

Throughout my struggle I felt the pain,
sitting by my window contemplating on a dull day as it rains,
my mind's overthinking giving me the strain,
at times I can't work it out in my brain so how do I explain?
what do I do?
looking for someone I can talk to,
is there anyone with whom I can relate?
I sit alone finish off what is left on my plate,
I feel no one cares,
God knows how I'll fare,
as I look and glare not wanting to be here
people look and think 'stay clear',
when I want to look out to a soul to share.

Caught up in my ways searching hard for brighter days,
Lord help me in my ways I want to maintain,
so I can feel again,
stressed enough as it is I'm off track wanting
to find the essence I had way back.

Whether its defence or attack,
I could handle all of his to that,
yet this is where I'm at.

Days pass, I slowly pick myself up and out,
It's hard and feels a struggle, yet I try and I do get about,
being true knowing what I have whether it's a little gain,
I've got to maintain,

with whatever is forthcoming I will try to sustain.
Seeking help believing I can pull through,
realising I can't rely on others to help me
and looking to others to help me pull through,
when it is all down to me, wanting to be,
relying on me to get me by, try stop asking why,
looking high,
I hope one day to reach the sky.

For whatever I have been through
will only make me stronger,
even if it takes me longer,
I still have a hunger burning first I will learn from this,
then I will see what I can earn from this.

Days get clearer as I pass
Keep my head up, don't lose the will to try
keep going, when I'm feeling low
Some moments I fear, still giving things a go
yet I prepare to take it on to see it clear,
rising above myself breezing through like air,
I am now reaching to there,
set down my goals
make them realistic
goals that I can grasp in my flow.

From the start I begin wanting to win, being patient,
steady as I progress, moving forward I press,
witnessing myself get to a stage,
where now I express it on a page.

Thinking not dwelling from when my thoughts were whack,
now I am on top can't no one hold me back,
not planning to stop reaching to higher levels,
which I can attain, believing in myself knowing I can achieve,
doing what I got to do, not waiting on them they or you.

From now on, watch where I be, moving steadily,
if I want to make anything out of me,
When I feel a hunger, I battle through the dark nights,
knowing there is brighter days pending in my sight.

Relations

Whether it is family or friends,
we all need some form of relation
in a world that seems to be separating,
caring for thyself alone,
getting what you own,
don't care for another, is what is told and also shown.

Describing families, wealthy or poor,
what are we all living for?
just to show disrespect to each other
showing little consideration for one another
what, do you feel a sensation,
out of segregating oneself from a sister or brother,
whether it is a family relation or not,
you are treating in a way,
that is breaking a trust,
which takes time for us to gain,
once a relations trust, is over,
the odds to maintain the relationship suffer
what do you gain in times of difficulty and pain?

We need support showing courtesy with people we truly see,
as ones who will empathise truly,
and be there when you need a soul to care,
instead of looking to the sky breathing the air
realising there is no one with whom you can share.

People

Look at the city reflect on what you see,
it is becoming a sour site,
people dread walking the streets after a certain time of night,
they feel restricted afraid,
dealers getting paid,
others afflicted with misery,
suffering due to the state they we in.

Hurt, alone, lost weather getting cold as people turn cold,
strangers in desperation looking for a smoke to burn,
people turn to direct and expect,
use force to get,
leaving lives devastated, with lost ones,
a life of regret and sorrow,
addicts begging to borrow,
no one seems to think,
wake up people will we see a tomorrow,
which of us is for sure, only the Lord knows.

As we pass on by showing no concern,
envying these days, is natural to people as is breathing,
quarrels in the home, in the clubs,
people in different mindsets,
others pranking on the streets and on the phones,
others sly deceivingly in your face,
no one there to help a poor soul who is in hunger,
or finding it hard as they are on their own,
families drifting apart,
lack of love in people's hearts,

loved ones depart over petty issues,
can't work it out,
now finding life hard to get about.

Ignorance and stubbornness, prevails,
to play its part,
characteristics which are inflicted to distract and mislead,
many of whom now follow that lead, where do we go,
not knowing turning to others who are caught up in the same flow,
others know yet no one shows another which way to go.

Even by showing a little empathy or consideration,
a little concern, that way benefits, for we earn,
yet selfishness covers us so,
life is tough, at times we all have it rough,
doing less of what you do is not enough,
take time to help one another,
for a time will come when you need one another,
never forget where you have come from,
always remember we will soon all be gone,
it may not be long.

Although it may not seem that way,
show someone the way,
make one feel a brighter day, times ticking,
soon the bones will be clicking,
do good in deeds and indeed you will succeed.
It is up to us as individuals,
to make a difference,
do not and surely a time will come where we plead,
it will be more than an instance.

The Streetz

Look at how we be living free,
yet open your eyes to see,
observe the city streets,
what do you like what you happen to see,
lives being taken away from night to day,
people hoping to see the next day,
others getting away from all,
no respite for the innocent as they fall,
just groups who feel they belong wanting to ball,
as they repel against one another,
their close families dwell in a hell,
when its time they are told things are not very well,
lives lost through actions of animosity,
among fellow brothers and sisters,
the use of guns and knives mixed with drugs and alcohol,
actions of the foolish and ignorant.

No thoughts for mothers who watch their loved ones grow,
as they feel loss as its them mothers who die slow,
with each day a burden of hurt that will never pass away,
People scared to walk the streets alone,
feel insecure going into certain codes or area zones,
merciless acts over petty pacts,
people react,
shook,
leaving them not knowing how to act,
due to the impact.

Yet revenge pends on,
it seems it will carry on as time passes on by,
leaving people gazing upon the skies
deceased members gone over envy and lies,
from enmity to those who despise,
families cry asking why,
no chance of a goodbye.

Led by anger and pride,
taking others wanting to be,
allowing evil temptations,
to instigate how they go forth,
when its minds manipulated with ideations
to plan killing others with no regret or remorse,
is this a course to take?
for eventually you end up making your own break,
whether six feet down, or in a prison cell, for your own sake.

For some of whom later as years have wasted on by,
some realise open their eyes,
contemplate even reflect,
on how it all came to be chilling as youths wanting to be,
influenced by peers, for whatever reason, from a grudge,
end up taking lives over whom you or others despised.

Now do you see,
any sense or is the evil impact on you too immense,
as you will recompense.

Eternal Seeds

A new year starts,
people are all drifting apart,
quicker than a flying dart reaching its destination,
for people burning in envy over a simple conversation,
while not looking to others or giving thanks
when brothers and sisters dying in deprivation.

Signs of fading nations,
all depleted lost in materialisation,
no love, care, or concerns on how we fare,
this is a state, a condition,
where people seem to be on a mission,
to get another down, leave them first to frown,
next to smile to them down,
yeah yes, you have a crown.

Thinking themselves as wise,
like they have some prize,
by the telling of lies,
their hearts despise,
you can see it burning in their eyes,
so what will rise after your lies?
a constant hunger to despise,
so you like to burn,
I see it well when you show concern,
looking at you when you turn,
for what is it you gain?
you are steady in your ways aiming to maintain,

envy and jealousy depleted in vain,
all the while you cannot refrain.

Ask yourself, what your actions will be,
small time moments of fake gain,
where in due time it is you who will suffer the pain,
fear the Lord for he knows of what you do,
in your state can you be true,
to those around you,
when you resent on all statements,
laugh at judgements made by fellow sisters and brothers,
like a minister, who dwells as a sinister,
not seeking to change, or rearrange,
not contemplating, just wanting to antagonise,
seeing people react amused with enmity, no empathy?

Take heed turn to the Lord what else can save you?
how long do you wish or plan to go on,
with those around you?
with all of what you do,
you need to find another path,
for you are facing the Lord's wrath,
heading into destruction,
for now you doing it without instruction,
get down seek forgiveness, or dwell depleted.

For soon you end up forgotten, well aware
that there's nobody there to care,
just burning buddies who will die miserably and slow,
all the while looking like a bad show.

What Do We Do?

It is a world out there ticking by with no care,
whether you are here or there,
in despair or whether its smiles everywhere,
people pass on by, try…then hope gazing to the sky,
people lie others cry, some ask why.

Was grafting a trade to gain a skill,
hoping it would serve me still,
thinking about what to write on your will,
relaxing at friends using time to chill,
going to theme parks to enjoy the thrill.

Looking around people, suffering pain, while others gain,
some refrain, some try maintain,
there are those who go insane,
not long until they make gains to better themselves again,
feeling the strain, on your long journey back on the train,
unblock the drain, caught at the bus stop
with no shelter in heavy rain,
feeling down, want to complain.

Progressing within, persevering, not giving in,
you out or you in?
people knowingly committing sin,
cut out the nicotine, going all out for the win.
Others trying hard to work it out,
some teach you how to get about,
scream then shout, walkabout,
at college or university want to drop out.

Rely on you, picking the book from the shelf,
getting into prayer,
knowing there is a Lord who forever cares.

Reading to revise it through,
moments are good to share,
thinking of moving on,
how many times are you going to listen to the same song?

In search of a place to go, feeling low,
fears to tears, people in arrears
driving instructor giving you an ear,
wrong gear,
restaurant or home, you enjoying the biryani,
spicy, add a green tea,
sometimes just let things just be,
get high, feeling fly, observing who passes on by,
handling your cash, next it's the car crash,
quick to dash, looking at a place to slash.

In love with the dove,
she is up above or always by your side,
enjoying the sun with your feet at the tide,
good to take a break,
along with some fun,
at a funfair what a ride,
disagree then agree,
work at it, they may still be a possibility,
stress mounting take it easy, give to a charity.

Take a drive down town to head to the meeting to greet,
who you been expecting to meet,
from birth joys to cuddly toys,
funerals to removals,
it is been a while since you last dialled,
how you been? Seen,
hook up with the team,
play some cards, don't forget to send a postcard,
there lays a man looking for some change,
practising golf to find a better range,
business plans wanting to rearrange.

I have thought a little while what the world can bring,
maybe I have reminded you of a thing,
one day the phone may ring, push the baby in its swing,
even surprise your lady, buy her a ring,
or wait for the bell when it finally rings,
got to be doing something,
I'm out of here, ding ding.

Parents

Be kind,
although at times it may seem, the love is blind,
with them lies unconditional love,
for whatever concern deep down,
they never mind, always there to remind,
for they raised you with hard effort,
so you feel ease and comfort,
true to you, not wanting to see you in discomfort,
taking you to resorts,
sharing their points of view,
helping take care of you,
to show you love and care,
aiding your way, guiding so you don't sway,
assisting you to prepare for a world out there,
that at times seems unclear.

Yet they strived to keep you going,
at times when you are not knowing,
for you, they end up showing.
Some of whom are fortunate mother and father besides,
in all of what you do, be thankful,
yet there are those that look to one,
others just have memories of their lost ones,
reflecting back on their presence can be a hard one.

Look at How We Be

Times are changing rapidly,
yet we blinded to see,
accept on how we see living ignorantly.

Don't see times are changing,
we end up rearranging without focusing
on what we got to be focusing upon,
instead hand in your coupon,
hoping not to wait too long,
as we carry on, strolling along,
we prolong listening to the same song,
following others in their ways to feel we belong.

Yet with all the signs,
combining the worldwide outlook,
seeing people's actions, people shook,
witnessing ruins,
conditions a state,
showing signs of an end that's coming at a sudden rate,
we don't see it is coming as its running.

Watching the TV, open your eyes,
your mind to what you see,
it sure as hell ain't pretty,
glad to be living free, letting things just be,
at times we forget how lucky we seem to be.
Others making mockery ignorantly
of other's lives unnecessarily.

Casually giving no care or thoughts
to our brothers and sisters.
We are all a nation yet have disputes leading to separation,
lack of communication on all fronts,
no dedication to the books, lack of understanding,
there are men and women of knowledge,
yet the men and women of knowledge are disregarded,
what can be expected in a world where,
the wise are rejected?
there is no prize,
just those who despise,
telling of many lies,
for what purpose? I ask,
the doors will soon close, well,
times ever so near…okay so…you do not care,
you think you see things clear?
too tied to the material, no time to prepare,
you don't give two craps on how you will fare,
who are you going to run to,
when time is upon us here,?
What, are you just going to glare,
like a breeze of air flowing through your hair?
time is upon us!
whether you here, there and could not give a care,
this is the time, prepare for you end up forgotten.

My message to you is for all of you all,
who want to see the Lord's might,
on a beautiful night,
reminiscing on the glory of a world that no soul has seen,
recognising a dream, there are those, who will be witnessing,
a victorious team, living in a mother of a dream,
yet why we do not believe what we see?
look at how we be. Do it eagerly from the heart, sincerely,
or you will not see…like many.

People Part 11

Observe what you happen to see walk down the street,
even those you meet,
spend time, even take note,
of what you hear upon the TV
looking at people's ways and displays,
what picture do you see?
or do you pass on by not concerned by what you see?
arrogant many ignorant,
there are people who lack mutual tolerance
over simple situations
what do you see? People with different communities
with diverse values?
many different beliefs?

Yet people concern themselves,
in groups of hatred and jealousy,
those who hypocritically pursue also attack others,
as people stand to watch in disbelief,
at what they are witnessing in front of their eyes in sheer grief,
as people neglect morals,
do not care what is wrong,
find it hard to do right,
keep to their own stubbornness,
to get what they want, or please,
while another brother falls to his knees, to plead,
only a few take heed.

Controlled by the passions of their inner greed,
minds over-influenced by the effects of drugs and alcohol,
leaving people to do as they desire,
so much disparity,
no love or concerns,
no pity, how then is there room for a little equality,
among people with too many differences between them?

No one takes or considers, another's point of view,
within groups there is too much separation,
many without relation,
leading to isolation,
will you or can you fit in?
even families lack equality among brothers and sisters,
general communities,
wherever you look, you witness those shook.

Lonely, afraid in despair,
lack of understanding, peace and sympathy towards one another,
so how and when is it possible for a kind of unity?
only when there is sincerity and wholehearted dedication
to the one true Lord,
God's morality which we should seek in guides,
books and in those who are seeking too,
will we then gain a devotion,
to others along with being more loving and tolerant,
will we find a little ease to being more peaceful to one another,
brothers to sisters, mothers and fathers.

To the youth among us,
will we then come to a stage of solidarity,
inclining to more good actions in these days
and age we are lacking on all fronts.

Yet we need to start with the elders who hold responsibility,
showing examples to the youth, ponder upon the skies,
remind ourselves of the Most Mighty and Most High.

Ask and search for guidance, the Lord above, Knower of all,
witnesses your efforts, those true and sincere,
The Lord sees you clear,
be among those good and fair,
time is running,
we all witnessing how times are becoming,
maybe a few,
as it time passes look among you,
how many do you see who are true?

Times We Are Living In

For times we living in,
confusion, hate and fear,
where are those who are sincere.

We are deluded, no time to give to family,
never mind friend,
even when they are close to an end.

No one seems to make anything clear,
we lose those to us dear,
why cannot anyone be true and show a little care?
we are all a race,
all given a place,
we cannot settle to respect one another,
war in the home between sister and brother,
while mother and father at each other's throats,
people watch and take note, gloat.

What is to happen for our youth?
who we give examples to,
among those who are growing today,
for they are to follow in our ways.

As some people pray for better days,
increases of people fighting across the planet,
as they commit,
themselves to take lives,
then pause to intermit.

Times seem as though may get worse,
wherever you look people are shook,
am I wrong? Lives in devastation across the globe,
little investigations, false accusations,
families forced to live in separation.

Far away from the feeling of contentment and bliss,
they are taking extremes when taking a form of destruction
into their own hands,
corrupt they may be, ignorantly living arrogantly,
those on top, let things pass away,
making their own paths clear,
sorting their own security.

For believe what you will,
time is upon us still,
still there is no reflection of what life is becoming,
what is forthcoming.

Every individual must realise through the coming times
that we can no longer let time go to waste,
prepare in your ways, seek a true path,
they the good old days have fled,
in the future they may be days
where events will lead us to dread,
for some of us not looking forward to those days ahead.

For time is coming upon us all,
Let us face it,
can we evade?
for the sun might be shining, yet will we enjoy a little shade,
asking for a respite, which one of us,
is going to sleep at night, struggle with it maybe,
turn to the Lord,
for He holds the key,
the Most High, for He enables each being to be,
search for the oneness to truly see.

Ask yourself

Why is there so much hate and disparity?
no love or unity,
people afraid to look up to see,
this life a sorrowful place to be,
ask yourself how you are,
why is that person so far,
for we together in this still no unity, there is no bliss.

Aiming with guns and tongues,
deadly it ends,
as people make amends,
reaching out to those,
from friends to those foes,
what lies ahead,
do we know?

Where has the guidance gone?
in past times it prolonged,
where do we all go wrong?
following ways to feel we belong.

Try working together,
for the good you do will show forever,
we need to guide,
put aside the pride,
help those to remind,
track back to pull forward those behind.

Aid other's ways, instead of hypocritical displays,
we all sway, in need of self-inspection in case we lose direction,
we are all sisters and brothers,
we need to focus on our intentions,
to purify our minds,
to help others not to reject,
a change is needed from us all,
not just to party, brawl and mouth,
show some courtesy instead of neglect with animosity.

There is always hope, cling to the rope,
we need each other more than we know,
witness the negativity replace it with positive activity,
to guide those of us in need,
cut out the selfishness along with the stubbornness,
bring out happiness.

Show some light in these dark days to nights,
what is there for our youth, if this prolongs?
the same old story,
disgrace to disaster,
a world that is ending faster.

We are all in need of change, find a different range,
to set about how you go forth,
for this is our lives at worth,
it is down to use all,
we are the masters of our downfall,
whether we are high or low,
we all want to fly to a more peaceful flow.

About the Author

Raja Zahid Khan was born in East London and raised in Handsworth, Birmingham. He currently works in Mental Health and enjoys writing poetry turning life into words and lines with hints of rhymes as a hobby. He is especially interested in writing poetry as a commentary for a lot of the issues we face in today's society.

Entering a poetry competition and getting published, encouraged him to take poetry further. Although life and health have played its part, producing and getting this book out is an achievement for Raja Zahid Khan and he intends to make a difference and share these poems so they can be appreciated by those who choose to read.

Be the author of your own destiny

Find out about our authors, events, services
and how you too can get your book journey started.

- Conscious Dreams Publishing
- @DreamsConscious
- @consciousdreamspublishing
- Daniella Blechner
- www.consciousdreamspublishing.com
- info@consciousdreamspublishing.com

Let's connect

Lightning Source UK Ltd.
Milton Keynes UK
UKHW010629050820
367737UK00001B/220